D1387869

ESSENTIAL
Puddings

p

Contents

Introduction

It was not until the seventeenth century that the pudding assumed its modern form as the sweet dish which follows a main meal. In fact the word 'pudding' originally applied to all dishes that had been boiled. Nowadays everyone generally knows and loves the pudding as the sweet last course. Yet a few exceptions still remain like Steak and Kidney Pudding, however most could not imagine eating this substantial dish after their main meal.

For those with a sweet tooth the pudding is the most anticipated and most delicious part of the meal. If you want to make a quick-and-easy pudding for the family fruit dishes are always popular. You could try Red Fruits with Foaming Sauce for example – a blend of redcurrants, strawberries and cranberries cooked with cinnamon, sugar and apple juice served with a tangy raspberry and marshmallow sauce. This dish could not be any simpler yet is absolutely delicious.

If you are a chocolate lover but always feel guilty after eating it, Chocolate Cheese Pots are the puddings for you. Not only is this sweet dish low in fat but it is full of chocolate flavour too. Obviously eating too much of most foods can cause health problems. Indeed, cocoa butter in chocolate contains saturated fat which can increase blood cholesterol levels. Recent research however, carried out at the University of California, has shown that chocolate (like red wine) contains high levels of chemicals known as phenolics. The research indicates that there are encouraging signs that these chemicals may be able to help lower the risk of heart disease. This is great news for lovers of chocolate desserts, but like all good things chocolate should only be eaten in moderation.

If you really want to impress and indulge your family and friends with a wonderful pudding, complete your meal by serving a Coconut Cream Tart. It takes a little time to prepare a good tart but the end result will be worth it, especially when filled with juicy pineapple, creamy coconut and wonderful whipped cream.

These dishes are just some of the recipes featured in this book, however all of the puddings included are exceptionally tasty and flavoursome. The recipes featured recreate traditional family favourites combined with modern dishes which use contemporary ingredients. As the saying goes, 'the proof of the pudding is in the eating', so why not give yourself a treat and serve pudding today.

Paper-thin Fruit Pies

Serves 4

INGREDIENTS

1 medium eating (dessert) apple	4 rectangular sheets of filo pastry, thawed if frozen	2 tsp icing (confectioner's) sugar, for dusting
1 medium ripe pear	2 tbsp low-sugar apricot jam	low-fat custard, to serve
2 tbsp lemon juice	1 tbsp unsweetened orange juice	
60 g/2 oz low-fat spread		

1 Preheat the oven to 200°C/400°F/Gas Mark 6. Core and thinly slice the apple and pear and toss them in the lemon juice to prevent discoloration.

2 Melt the low-fat spread over a gentle heat.

3 Cut the sheets of pastry into 4 and cover with a clean, damp tea towel (dish cloth). Brush 4 non-stick Yorkshire pudding tins (large muffin pans), measuring 10 cm/4 inch across, with a little of the low-fat spread.

4 Working on each pie separately, brush 4 sheets of pastry with the melted low-fat spread. Press a small sheet of pastry into the base of one tin (pan). Arrange the other sheets of pastry on top at slightly different angles. Repeat with the other sheets of pastry to make another 3 pies.

5 Arrange the apple and pear slices alternately in the centre of each pastry case and lightly crimp the edges of the pastry of each pie.

6 Mix the apricot jam and orange juice together until smooth and generously brush over the fruit. Bake for 12–15 minutes. Dust with icing (confectioner's) sugar and serve hot with low-fat custard.

VARIATION

Other combinations of fruit are equally delicious. Try peach and apricot, raspberry and apple, or pineapple and mango.

Almond Trifles

Serves 4

INGREDIENTS

8 Amaretti di Saronno biscuits	300 ml/^{1}/$_2$ pint/1^1/$_4$ cups	1 tsp almond essence (extract)
4 tbsp brandy or Amaretti	low-fat custard	15 g/^{1}/$_2$ oz toasted almonds,
liqueur	300 ml/^{1}/$_2$ pint/1^1/$_4$ cups low-	flaked (slivered)
225 g/8 oz raspberries	fat natural fromage frais	1 tsp cocoa powder
	(unsweetened yogurt)	

1 Place the biscuits in a mixing bowl and using the end of a rolling pin, carefully crush the biscuits into small pieces.

2 Divide the crushed biscuits among 4 serving glasses. Sprinkle the brandy or liqueur over the crushed biscuits and leave to stand for about 30 minutes to allow the biscuits to soften.

3 Top the layer of crushed biscuits with a layer of raspberries, reserving a few raspberries for decoration, and spoon over enough custard to just cover.

4 Mix the fromage frais (unsweetened yogurt) with the almond essence (extract) and spoon over the custard. Leave to chill in the refrigerator for about 30 minutes.

5 Just before serving, sprinkle over the toasted almonds and dust with cocoa powder. Decorate with the reserved raspberries and serve at once.

VARIATION

Try this trifle with assorted summer fruits. If they are a frozen mix, use them frozen and allow them to thaw so that the juices soak into the biscuit base – it will taste truly delicious.

Almond & Sultana Cheesecakes

Serves 4

INGREDIENTS

12 Amaretti di Saronno
  biscuits
1 medium egg white, beaten
225 g/8 oz skimmed-milk soft
  cheese
$^1/_2$ tsp almond essence
  (extract)

$^1/_2$ tsp finely grated lime rind
25 g/1 oz ground almonds
25 g/1 oz caster (superfine)
  sugar
60 g/2 oz sultanas
2 tsp powdered gelatine
2 tbsp boiling water

2 tbsp lime juice

TO DECORATE:
25 g/1 oz flaked (slivered)
  toasted almonds
strips of lime rind

1 Preheat the oven to 180°C/350°F/Gas Mark 4. Place the biscuits in a clean plastic bag, seal the bag and using a rolling pin, crush them into small pieces. Place the crumbs in a bowl and bind together with the egg white.

2 Arrange 4 non-stick pastry rings or poached egg rings, 9 cm/3½ inches across, on a baking sheet (cookie sheet) lined with baking parchment. Divide the biscuit mixture into 4

equal portions and spoon it into the rings, pressing down well. Bake for 10 minutes until crisp and leave to cool in the rings.

3 Beat together the soft cheese, almond essence (extract), lime rind, ground almonds, sugar and sultanas until well mixed.

4 Dissolve the gelatine in the boiling water and stir in the lime juice. Fold into the cheese mixture and spoon over the biscuit

bases. Smooth over the tops and chill for 1 hour until set.

5 Loosen the cheesecakes using a small palette knife (spatula) and transfer to serving plates. Decorate with toasted almonds and lime rind, and serve.

VARIATION

If you prefer, substitute chopped no-need-to-soak dried apricots for the sultanas.

Red Fruits with Foaming Sauce

Serves 4

INGREDIENTS

225 g/8 oz redcurrants,
  washed and trimmed,
  thawed if frozen
225 g/8 oz cranberries
75 g/3 oz light muscovado
  sugar

200 ml/7 fl oz/³/4 cup
  unsweetened apple juice
1 cinnamon stick, broken
300 g/10¹/2 oz small
  strawberries, washed,
  hulled and halved

SAUCE:
225 g/8 oz raspberries, thawed
  if frozen
2 tbsp fruit cordial
100 g/3¹/2 oz marshmallows

1 Place the redcurrants, cranberries and sugar in a saucepan. Pour in the apple juice and add the cinnamon stick. Bring the mixture to the boil and simmer gently for 10 minutes until the fruit has just softened.

2 Stir the strawberries into the cranberry and sugar mixture and mix well. Transfer the mixture to a bowl, cover and leave to chill for about 1 hour. Remove and discard the cinnamon stick.

3 Just before serving, make the sauce. Place the raspberries and fruit cordial in a small pan, bring to the boil and simmer for 2–3 minutes until the fruit is just beginning to soften. Stir the marshmallows into the raspberry mixture and heat through, stirring, until the marshmallows begin to melt.

4 Transfer the fruit salad to serving bowls. Spoon over the raspberry and marshmallow sauce and serve.

VARIATION

This sauce is delicious poured over low-fat ice cream. For an extra-colourful sauce, replace the raspberries with an assortment of summer berries.

Brown Bread Ice Cream

Serves 4

INGREDIENTS

175 g/6 oz fresh wholemeal
breadcrumbs
25 g/1 oz finely chopped
walnuts
60 g/2 oz caster (superfine)
sugar

$1/2$ tsp ground nutmeg
1 tsp finely grated orange rind
450 ml/16 fl oz/2 cups low-fat
natural (unsweetened)
yogurt
2 large egg whites

TO DECORATE:
walnut halves
orange slices
fresh mint leaves

1 Preheat the grill (broiler) to medium. Mix the breadcrumbs, walnuts and sugar together and spread over a sheet of foil in the grill (broiler) pan. Grill (broil), stirring frequently, for 5 minutes until crisp and evenly browned. (Take care that the sugar does not burn.) Remove from the heat and leave to cool.

2 When cool, transfer to a mixing bowl and mix in the nutmeg, orange rind and yogurt. In another bowl, whisk the egg whites until stiff. Gently fold into the breadcrumb mixture, using a metal spoon.

3 Spoon the mixture into 4 mini-basins, smooth over the tops and freeze for $1^{1}/2$–2 hours until firm.

4 To serve, hold the bases of the moulds (molds) in hot water for a few seconds, then turn out on to serving plates. Serve immediately, decorated with walnut halves, orange slices and fresh mint leaves.

COOK'S TIP

If you don't have mini-basins, use ramekins or teacups or, if you prefer, use one large bowl. Alternatively, spoon the mixture into a large, freezing container to freeze and serve the ice cream in scoops.

Chocolate Cheese Pots

Serves 4

INGREDIENTS

300 ml/^{1}/$_2$ pint/1^1/$_4$ cups low-
fat natural fromage frais
(unsweetened yogurt)
150 ml/5 fl oz/^{2}/$_3$ cup low-fat
natural (unsweetened)
yogurt

25 g/1 oz icing (confectioner's)
sugar
4 tsp low-fat drinking
chocolate powder
4 tsp cocoa powder
1 tsp vanilla essence (extract)
2 tbsp dark rum (optional)

2 medium egg whites
4 chocolate cake decorations

TO SERVE:
pieces of kiwi fruit, orange
and banana
strawberries and raspberries

1 Combine the fromage frais (unsweetened yogurt) and low-fat yogurt in a mixing bowl. Sift in the sugar, drinking chocolate and cocoa powder and mix well. Add the vanilla essence (extract) and rum, if using.

2 In another bowl, whisk the egg whites until stiff. Using a metal spoon, fold the egg whites into the fromage frais (unsweetened yogurt) and chocolate mixture.

3 Spoon the fromage frais (unsweetened yogurt) and chocolate mixture into 4 small china dessert pots and leave to chill for about 30 minutes. Decorate each chocolate cheese pot with a chocolate cake decoration.

4 Serve each chocolate cheese pot with an assortment of fresh fruit, such as pieces of kiwi fruit, orange and banana, and a few whole strawberries and raspberries.

VARIATION

This chocolate mixture would make an excellent filling for a cheesecake. Make the base out of crushed Amaretti di Saronno biscuits and egg white, and set the filling with 2 tsp powdered gelatine dissolved in 2 tbsp boiling water. Make sure you use biscuits made from apricot kernels, which are virtually fat free.

Tropical Fruit Fool

Serves 4

INGREDIENTS

1 medium ripe mango
2 kiwi fruit
1 medium banana
2 tbsp lime juice

$^1/_2$ tsp finely grated lime rind,
plus extra to decorate
2 medium egg whites
425 g/15 oz can low-fat
custard

$^1/_2$ tsp vanilla essence
(extract)
2 passion fruit

1 To peel the mango, slice either side of the smooth, flat central stone. Roughly chop the flesh and blend the fruit in a food processor or blender until smooth. Alternatively, mash the chopped mango flesh with a fork.

2 Peel the kiwi fruit, chop the flesh into small pieces and place in a bowl. Peel and chop the banana and add to the bowl. Toss all of the fruit in the lime juice and rind and mix well to prevent discoloration.

3 In a grease-free bowl, whisk the egg whites until stiff and then gently fold in the custard and vanilla essence (extract) until thoroughly mixed.

4 In 4 tall glasses, alternately layer the chopped fruit, mango purée and custard mixture, finishing with the custard on top. Leave to chill in the refrigerator for 20 minutes.

5 Halve the passion fruits, scoop out the seeds and spoon the passion fruit over the fruit fools.

6 Decorate each serving with the extra lime rind and serve.

VARIATION

Other tropical fruits to try include papaya purée, with chopped pineapple and dates, and tamarillo or pomegranate seeds to decorate. Or make a summer fruit fool by using strawberry purée, topped with raspberries and blackberries, with cherries to finish.

Fruit & Fibre Layers

Serves 4

INGREDIENTS

115 g/4 oz no-need-to-soak dried apricots	60g /2 oz dried apple	1 cinnamon stick, broken
115 g/4 oz no-need-to-soak dried prunes	25 g/1 oz dried cherries	300 ml/$^{1}/_{2}$ pint/1$^{1}/_{4}$ cups low-fat natural yogurt
115 g/4 oz no-need-to-soak dried peaches	450 ml/16 fl oz/2 cups unsweetened apple juice	115 g/4 oz crunchy oat cereal
	6 cardamom pods	apricot slices, to decorate
	6 cloves	

1 To make the fruit compote, place the dried apricots, prunes, peaches, apples and cherries in a saucepan and pour in the apple juice.

2 Add the cardamom pods, cloves and cinnamon stick to the pan, bring to the boil and simmer for 10–15 minutes until the fruits are plump and tender.

3 Leave the mixture to cool completely in the pan. Remove and discard the spices from the fruits, then transfer the mixture to a bowl and leave to chill in the refrigerator for 1 hour.

4 Spoon the compote into 4 dessert glasses, layering it alternately with yogurt and oat cereal, finishing with the oat cereal on top.

5 Decorate each dessert with slices of apricot and serve at once.

COOK'S TIP

There are many dried fruits available, including mangoes and pears, some of which need soaking, so read the instructions on the packet before use. Also, check the ingredients label, because several types of dried fruit have added sugar or are rolled in sugar, and this will affect the sweetness of the dish that you use them in.

Pan-cooked Apples in Red Wine

Serves 4

INGREDIENTS

4 eating (dessert) apples
2 tbsp lemon juice
40 g/1^1/2 oz low-fat spread
60 g/2 oz light muscovado
    sugar

1 small orange
1 cinnamon stick, broken
150 ml/5 fl oz/^{2}/3 cup red
    wine

225 g/8 oz raspberries, hulled
    and thawed if frozen
sprigs of fresh mint, to
    decorate

1 Peel and core the apples, then cut them into thick wedges. Place the apples in a bowl and toss in the lemon juice to prevent the fruit from discoloring.

2 In a frying pan (skillet), gently melt the low-fat spread over a low heat, add the sugar and stir to form a paste.

3 Stir the apple wedges into the pan and cook, stirring occasionally, for 2 minutes until well coated in the sugar paste.

4 Using a vegetable peeler, pare off a few strips of orange rind. Add the orange rind to the pan along with the cinnamon pieces. Extract the juice from the orange and pour into the pan with the red wine. Bring to the boil, then simmer for 10 minutes, stirring.

5 Add the raspberries to the pan and cook for 5 minutes until the apples are tender.

6 Discard the orange rind and cinnamon

pieces. Transfer the apple and raspberry mixture to a serving plate together with the wine sauce. Decorate with a sprig of fresh mint and serve hot.

VARIATION

For other fruity combinations, cook the apples with blackberries, blackcurrants or redcurrants. You may need to add more sugar if you use currants as they are not as sweet as raspberries.

Mixed Fruit Brûlées

Serves 4

INGREDIENTS

450 g/1 lb prepared, assorted
summer fruits (such as
strawberries, raspberries,
blackcurrants, redcurrants
and cherries), thawed if
frozen

150 ml/5 fl oz/³/4 cup half-fat
double (heavy) cream
alternative
150 ml/5 fl oz/³/4 cup low-fat
natural fromage frais
(unsweetened yogurt)

1 tsp vanilla essence (extract)
4 tbsp demerara (brown
crystal) sugar

1 Divide the
strawberries,
raspberries, blackcurrants,
redcurrants and cherries
evenly among 4 small,
heatproof ramekin dishes.

2 Mix together the half-
fat cream alternative,
fromage frais
(unsweetened yogurt) and
vanilla essence (extract).
Generously spoon the
mixture over the fruit.

3 Preheat the grill
(broiler) to hot. Top
each serving with

1 tablespoon demerara
(brown crystal) sugar and
grill (broil) the desserts
for 2–3 minutes, until the
sugar melts and begins to
caramelize. Serve hot.

VARIATION

*If you are making this
dessert for a special occasion,
soak the fruits in 2–3 tbsp
fruit liqueur before topping
with the cream mixture.*

COOK'S TIP

*Look out for half-fat creams,
in single and double (light
and heavy) varieties. They
are good substitutes for
occasional use. Alternatively,
in this recipe, omit the
cream and double the
quantity of fromage frais
(yogurt) for a lower
fat version.*

Grilled Fruit Platter with Lime 'Butter'

Serves 4

INGREDIENTS

1 baby pineapple
1 ripe papaya
1 ripe mango
2 kiwi fruit
4 apple (finger) bananas

4 tbsp dark rum
1 tsp ground allspice
2 tbsp lime juice
4 tbsp dark muscovado sugar

LIME 'BUTTER':
60 g/2 oz low-fat spread
1/2 tsp finely grated lime rind
1 tbsp icing (confectioner's)
sugar

1 Quarter the pineapple, trimming away most of the leaves, and place in a shallow dish. Peel the papaya, cut it in half and scoop out the seeds. Cut the flesh into thick wedges and place in the same dish as the pineapple.

2 Peel the mango, cut either side of the smooth, central flat stone and remove the stone. Slice the flesh into thick wedges. Peel the kiwi fruit and cut in half. Peel the bananas. Add all of these fruits to the dish.

3 Sprinkle over the rum, allspice and lime juice, cover and leave at room temperature for 30 minutes, turning occasionally, to allow the flavours to develop.

4 Meanwhile, make the 'butter'. Place the low-fat spread in a small bowl and beat in the lime rind and sugar until well mixed. Leave to chill in the refrigerator until required.

5 Preheat the grill (broiler) to hot. Drain the fruit, reserving the

juices, and arrange in the grill (broiler) pan. Sprinkle with the sugar and grill (broil) for 3–4 minutes until hot, bubbling and just beginning to char.

6 Transfer the fruit to a serving plate and spoon over the juices. Serve with the lime 'butter'.

VARIATION

Serve with a light sauce of 300 ml/ 1/2 pint/1 1/4 cups tropical fruit juice thickened with 2 tsp arrowroot.

White Lace Crêpes with Oriental Fruits

Serves 4

INGREDIENTS

3 medium egg whites	FRUIT FILLING:	1 cm/^{1}/2 inch piece root
4 tbsp cornflour (cornstarch)	350 g/12 oz fresh lychees	(fresh) ginger
3 tbsp cold water	^{1}/4 Galia melon	2 pieces stem ginger in syrup
1 tsp vegetable oil	175 g/6 oz seedless green	2 tbsp ginger wine or dry
	grapes	sherry

1. To make the fruit filling, peel the lychees and remove the stones. Place the lychees in a bowl. Scoop out the seeds from the melon and remove the skin. Cut the melon flesh into small pieces and place in the bowl.

2. Wash and dry the grapes, remove the stalks and add to the bowl. Peel the ginger and cut into thin shreds or grate finely. Drain the stem ginger pieces, reserving the syrup, and chop the ginger pieces quite finely.

3. Mix the gingers into the bowl along with the ginger wine or sherry and the reserved stem ginger syrup. Cover and set aside.

4. Meanwhile, prepare the crêpes. In a small jug, mix together the egg whites, cornflour (cornstarch) and cold water until very smooth.

5. Brush a small non-stick crêpe pan with oil and heat until hot. Drizzle the surface of the pan with a quarter of the cornflour (cornstarch) mixture to give a lacy effect. Cook for a few seconds until set, then carefully lift out and transfer to absorbent kitchen paper to drain. Set aside and keep warm. Repeat with the remaining mixture to make 4 crêpes in total.

6. To serve, place a crêpe on each serving plate and top with the fruit filling. Fold over the pancake and serve hot.

Banana & Lime Cake

Serves 10

INGREDIENTS

300 g/10^{1}/$_{2}$ oz plain (all-purpose) flour
1 tsp salt
1^{1}/$_{2}$ tsp baking powder
175 g/6 oz light muscovado sugar
1 tsp lime rind, grated
1 medium egg, beaten

1 medium banana, mashed with 1 tbsp lime juice
150 ml/5 fl oz/^{2}/$_{3}$ cup low-fat natural fromage frais (unsweetened yogurt)
115 g/4 oz sultanas
banana chips and finely grated lime rind, to decorate

TOPPING:
115 g/4 oz icing (confectioner's) sugar
1–2 tsp lime juice
^{1}/$_{2}$ tsp lime rind, finely grated

1 Preheat the oven to 180°C/350°F/Gas Mark 4. Grease and line a deep 18 cm/7 inch round cake tin (pan) with baking parchment. Sift the flour, salt and baking powder into a bowl and stir in the sugar and lime rind.

2 Make a well in the centre of the dry ingredients and add the egg, banana, fromage frais (yogurt) and sultanas. Mix well until incorporated.

3 Spoon the mixture into the tin and smooth the surface. Bake for 40–45 minutes until firm to the touch or until a skewer inserted in the centre comes out clean. Leave to cool for 10 minutes, then turn out on to a wire rack.

4 For the topping, sift the icing (confectioner's) sugar into a bowl and mix with the lime juice to form a soft, but not too runny, icing. Stir in the lime rind.

Drizzle the icing over the cake, letting it run down the sides.

5 Decorate with banana chips and lime rind. Let stand for 15 minutes so that the icing sets.

VARIATION

Replace the lime rind and juice with orange and the sultanas with chopped apricots.

Rich Fruit Cake

Serves 12

INGREDIENTS

175 g/6 oz unsweetened
pitted dates
115 g/4 oz no-need-to-soak
dried prunes
200 ml/7 fl oz/³/₄ cup
unsweetened orange juice
2 tbsp treacle (molasses)
1 tsp finely grated lemon rind
1 tsp finely grated orange rind

225 g/8 oz self-raising
wholemeal (whole wheat)
flour
1 tsp mixed spice
115 g/4 oz seedless raisins
115 g/4 oz golden sultanas
115 g/4 oz currants
115 g/4 oz dried cranberries
3 large eggs, separated

icing (confectioner's) sugar, to
dust

TO DECORATE:
1 tbsp apricot jam, softened
175 g/6 oz sugarpaste
strips of orange rind
strips of lemon rind

1 Preheat the oven to 170°C/325°F/Gas Mark 3. Grease and line a deep 20.5 cm/8 inch round cake tin (pan). Chop the dates and prunes and place in a pan. Pour over the orange juice and bring to the boil. Simmer for 10 minutes until very soft. Remove the pan from the heat and beat the fruit mixture until puréed. Stir in the treacle (molasses) and citrus rinds. Let cool.

2 Sift the flour and mixed spice into a bowl, adding any husks that remain in the sieve. Mix in the dried fruits and make a well in the centre.

3 When the date and prune mixture is cool, whisk in the egg yolks. In a separate bowl, whisk the egg whites until stiff. Spoon the fruit and egg yolk mixture into the dry ingredients and mix.

4 Fold in the egg whites using a metal spoon. Transfer to the tin (pan) and bake for 1½ hours. Leave to cool in the tin (pan).

5 Remove the cake from the tin (pan) and brush the top with jam. Dust the work surface with icing (confectioner's) sugar and roll out the sugarpaste thinly. Lay the sugarpaste over the top of the cake and trim the edges. Decorate.

Strawberry Roulade

Serves 8

INGREDIENTS

3 large eggs
115 g/4 oz caster (superfine)
sugar
115 g/4 oz plain (all-purpose)
flour
1 tbsp hot water

FILLING:
200 ml/7 fl oz/³/₄ cup low-fat
natural fromage frais
(unsweetened yogurt)
1 tsp almond essence (extract)
225 g/8 oz small strawberries

15 g/¹/₂ oz toasted almonds,
flaked (slivered)
1 tsp icing (confectioner's)
sugar

1 Preheat the oven to 220°C/425°F/Gas Mark 7. Line a 35 x 25 cm/ 14 x 10 inch Swiss roll tin (pan) with parchment. Place the eggs in a bowl with the caster (superfine) sugar. Place the bowl over a pan of hot water and whisk until pale and thick.

2 Remove the bowl from the pan. Sift in the flour and fold into the eggs with the hot water. Pour the mixture into the tin (pan) and bake for 8–10 minutes, until golden and set.

3 Transfer the mixture to a sheet of parchment. Peel off the lining paper and roll up the sponge along with the parchment. Wrap in a tea towel (dish towel) and let cool.

4 To make the filling, mix together the fromage frais (yogurt) and almond essence (extract). Reserving a few strawberries for decoration, wash, hull and slice the rest. Leave the filling mixture to chill until ready to assemble.

5 Unroll the sponge, spread the fromage frais (yogurt) mixture over the sponge and sprinkle with the strawberries. Roll the sponge up again. Sprinkle with the almonds and lightly dust with icing (confectioner's) sugar. Decorate with the reserved strawberries.

VARIATION

Serve the roulade with a fruit purée, sweetened with a little sugar.

Fruity Muffins

Makes 10

225 g/8 oz self-raising wholemeal (whole wheat) flour

2 tsp baking powder

25 g/1 oz light muscovado sugar

100 g/3$\frac{1}{2}$ oz no-need-to-soak dried apricots, chopped finely

1 medium banana, mashed with 1 tbsp orange juice

1 tsp orange rind, grated finely

300 ml/$\frac{1}{2}$ pint/1$\frac{1}{4}$ cups skimmed milk

1 medium egg, beaten

3 tbsp corn oil

2 tbsp porridge oats (oatmeal)

fruit spread, honey or maple syrup, to serve

1 Preheat the oven to 200°C/400°F/Gas Mark 6. Place 10 paper muffin cases in a deep patty tin (pan).

2 Sift the flour and baking powder into a bowl, adding any husks that remain in the sieve. Stir in the sugar and apricots.

3 Make a well in the centre of the dry ingredients and add the banana, orange rind, milk, beaten egg and oil. Mix to

form a thick batter. Divide the batter evenly among the 10 paper cases.

4 Sprinkle with a few porridge oats (oatmeal) and bake for 25–30 minutes until well risen and firm to the touch, or until a skewer inserted into the centre comes out clean. Transfer to a wire rack to cool slightly.

5 Serve the muffins warm with a little fruit spread, honey or maple syrup.

VARIATION

If you like dried figs, they make a deliciously crunchy alternative to the apricots; they also go very well with the flavour of orange. Other no-need-to-soak dried fruits, chopped up finely, can be used as well. Store these muffins in an airtight container for 3-4 days. They also freeze well in sealed bags or in freezer containers for up to 3 months.

Chocolate Brownies

Makes 12

INGREDIENTS

60 g/2 oz unsweetened pitted dates, chopped

60 g/2 oz no-need-to-soak dried prunes, chopped

6 tbsp unsweetened apple juice

4 medium eggs, beaten

300 g/10^1/2 oz dark muscovado sugar

1 tsp vanilla essence (extract)

4 tbsp low-fat drinking chocolate powder

2 tbsp cocoa powder

175 g/6 oz plain (all-purpose) flour

60 g/2 oz dark chocolate chips

ICING:

115 g/4 oz icing (confectioner's) sugar

1–2 tsp water

1 tsp vanilla essence (extract)

1 Preheat the oven to 180°C/350°F/Gas Mark 4. Grease and line a 18 x 28 cm/7 x 11 inch cake tin (pan) with parchment. Place the dates and prunes in a small pan and add the apple juice. Bring to the boil, cover and simmer for 10 minutes until soft. Beat to form a smooth paste, then set aside to cool.

2 Place the cooled fruit in a mixing bowl and stir in the eggs, sugar and vanilla essence. Sift in 4 tbsp drinking chocolate, the cocoa and the flour, and fold in along with the chocolate chips until well incorporated.

3 Spoon the mixture into the prepared tin (pan) and smooth over the top. Bake for 25–30 minutes until firm to the touch or until a skewer inserted into the centre comes out clean. Cut into 12 bars and leave to cool in the tin (pan) for

10 minutes. Transfer to a wire rack to cool completely.

4 To make the icing, sift the sugar into a bowl and mix with enough water and the vanilla essence (extract) to form a soft, but not too runny, icing.

5 Drizzle the icing over the chocolate brownies and allow to set. Dust with extra chocolate powder before serving.

Pavlova

Serves 6

INGREDIENTS

3 egg whites
pinch of salt
175 g/6 oz/^{3}/4 cup caster
(superfine) sugar

300 ml/^{1}/2 pint/1^1/4 cups
double (heavy) cream,
lightly whipped

fresh fruit of your choice
(raspberries, strawberries,
peaches, passion fruit, cape
gooseberries)

1 Line a baking sheet (cookie sheet) with a sheet of baking parchment.

2 Whisk the egg whites with the salt in a large bowl until soft peaks form.

3 Whisk in the sugar a little at a time, whisking well after each addition until all of the sugar has been incorporated.

4 Spoon three-quarters of the meringue on to the baking sheet (cookie sheet), forming a round 20 cm/8 inches in diameter.

5 Place spoonfuls of the remaining meringue all around the edge of the round so they join up to make a nest shape.

6 Bake in a preheated oven, 140°C/275°F/Gas Mark 1, for 1¼ hours.

7 Turn the heat off, but leave the pavlova in the oven until completely cold.

8 To serve, place the pavlova on a serving dish. Spread with the lightly whipped cream, then arrange the fresh fruit on top.

COOK'S TIP

It is a good idea to make the pavlova in the evening and leave it in the turned-off oven overnight.

Sticky Chocolate Pudding

Serves 6

INGREDIENTS

125 g/4¹/² oz/¹/² cup butter,
    softened
150 g/5¹/² oz/³/⁴ cup soft
    brown sugar
3 eggs, beaten
pinch of salt
25 g/1 oz cocoa powder

125 g/4¹/² oz/1 cup self-
    raising flour
25 g/1 oz dark chocolate,
    chopped finely
75 g/2³/⁴ oz white chocolate,
    chopped finely

SAUCE:
150 ml/5 fl oz/²/³ cup double
    (heavy) cream
75 g/2³/⁴ oz/¹/³ cup soft
    brown sugar
25 g/1 oz/6 tsp butter

1 Lightly grease 6 individual 175 ml/ 6 fl oz/³/⁴ cup pudding basins (molds).

2 Cream together the butter and sugar until pale and fluffy. Beat in the eggs a little at a time.

3 Sieve (strain) the salt, cocoa powder and flour into the creamed mixture and fold through the mixture. Stir the chopped chocolate evenly into the mixture.

4 Divide the mixture between the prepared pudding basins (molds). Lightly grease 6 squares of foil and use them to cover the basins (molds). Press around the edges to seal.

5 Place the basins (molds) in a roasting tin (pan) and add boiling water to come halfway up the sides of the basins (molds).

6 Bake in a preheated oven, 180°/350°F/Gas Mark 4, for 50 minutes, or until a skewer inserted into the centre comes out clean. Remove the basins (molds) from the tin and set aside.

7 To make the sauce, put the cream, sugar and butter into a pan and bring to the boil over a gentle heat. Simmer gently until the sugar has dissolved.

8 Turn the puddings out on to serving plates, pour the sauce over the top and serve immediately.

Fruit Crumble Tart

Serves 8

INGREDIENTS

PASTRY (PIE DOUGH):
150 g/5 oz/1¼ cups plain (all-purpose) flour
25 g/1 oz/5 tsp caster (superfine) sugar
125 g/4½ oz/½ cup butter, cut into small pieces
1 tbsp water

FILLING:
250 g/9 oz raspberries
450 g/1 lb plums, halved, stoned and chopped roughly
3 tbsp demerara (brown crystal) sugar

TO SERVE:
single (light) cream

TOPPING:
125 g/4½ oz/1 cup plain (all-purpose) flour
75 g/2¾ oz/⅓ cup demerara (brown crystal) sugar
100 g/3½ oz/½ cup butter, cut into small pieces
100 g/3½ oz chopped mixed nuts
1 tsp ground cinnamon

1 To make the pastry (pie dough), place the flour, sugar and butter in a bowl and rub in the butter with your fingers. Add the water and work the mixture together until a soft pastry (pie dough) has formed. Wrap and leave to chill for 30 minutes.

2 Roll out the pastry (pie dough) to line the base of a 24 cm/9½ inch loose-bottomed quiche/flan tin (pan). Prick the base of the pastry (pie dough) with a fork and leave to chill for about 30 minutes.

3 To make the filling, toss the raspberries and plums together with the sugar and spoon into the pastry case (pie shell).

4 To make the crumble topping, combine the flour, sugar and butter. Work the butter into the flour with your fingers until the mixture resembles coarse breadcrumbs. Stir in the nuts and cinnamon.

5 Sprinkle the topping over the fruit and bake in a preheated oven, 200°C/400°F/Gas Mark 6, for 20-25 minutes until golden. Serve the tart with single (light) cream.

Apple Tart Tatin

Serves 8

INGREDIENTS

125 g/4¹/₂ oz/¹/₂ cup butter
125 g/4¹/₂ oz/¹/₂ cup caster
  (superfine) sugar
4 dessert apples, cored and
  quartered

250 g/9 oz fresh ready-made
  shortcrust pastry (pie
  dough)

crème fraîche, to serve

1 Heat the butter and sugar in a 23 cm/9 inch ovenproof frying pan (skillet) over a medium heat for 5 minutes until the mixture begins to caramelize. Remove from the heat.

2 Arrange the apple quarters, skin side down, in the pan, taking care as the butter and sugar are very hot. Return the pan (skillet) to the heat and simmer for 2 minutes.

3 On a lightly floured surface, roll out the pastry (pie dough) to form a circle just a little larger than the pan.

4 Place the pastry (pie dough) over the apples, press down and tuck in the edges to seal the apples under the layer of pastry.

5 Bake in a preheated oven, 200°C/400°F/Gas Mark 6, for 20-25 minutes until golden. Remove from the oven and leave to cool for about 10 minutes.

6 Place a serving plate over the frying pan (skillet) and invert so that the pastry forms the base of the turned-out tart. Serve warm with crème fraîche.

VARIATION

Replace the apples with pears, if you prefer. Leave the skin on the pears, cut them into quarters and then remove the core.

Treacle Tart

Serves 8

INGREDIENTS

250 g/ 9 oz fresh ready-made
  shortcrust pastry
350 g/12 oz/1 cup golden
  (light corn) syrup
125 g/4^1/2 oz/2 cups fresh
  white breadcrumbs

125 ml/4 fl oz/^{1}/2 cup double
  (heavy) cream
finely grated rind of ^{1}/2 lemon
  or orange

2 tbsp lemon or orange juice
custard, to serve

1 Roll out the pastry
(pie dough) to line a
20 cm/8 inch loose-
bottomed quiche/flan tin
(pan), reserving the pastry
(pie dough) trimmings.
Prick the base of the pastry
(pie dough) with a fork and
leave to chill in the
refrigerator.

2 Using a shaped pastry
cutter or a sharp knife,
cut out small shapes from
the reserved pastry (pie
dough) trimmings, such as
leaves, stars or hearts, to
decorate the top of the tart.

3 In a bowl, mix together
the golden (light corn)
syrup, breadcrumbs, cream
and grated lemon or orange
rind and lemon or orange
juice.

4 Pour the mixture into
the pastry case (pie
shell) and decorate the
edges of the tart with the
pastry (pie dough) cut-outs.

5 Bake in a preheated
oven, 190°C/375°F/Gas
Mark 5, for 35-40 minutes
or until the filling
is just set.

6 Leave the tart to cool
slightly in the tin.
Turn out and serve with
custard.

VARIATION

*Use the pastry
(pie dough) trimmings to
create a lattice pattern on top
of the tart, if preferred.*

Orange Tart

Serves 6-8

INGREDIENTS

PASTRY (PIE DOUGH):
150 g/5 oz/1¼ cups plain (all-purpose) flour
25 g/1 oz/5 tsp caster (superfine) sugar
125 g /4½ oz/½ cup butter, cut into small pieces
1 tbsp water

FILLING:
grated rind of 2 oranges
9 tbsp orange juice
50 g/1¾ oz/⅞ cups fresh white breadcrumbs
2 tbsp lemon juice
150 ml/¼ pint/⅔ cup single (light) cream

50 g/1¾ oz/¼ cup butter
50 g/1¾ oz/¼ cup caster (superfine) sugar
2 eggs, separated
pinch of salt

1 To make the pastry (pie dough), place the flour and sugar in a bowl and rub in the butter. Add the cold water and work the mixture together until a soft pastry (pie dough) has formed. Wrap and leave to chill for 30 minutes.

2 Roll out the dough and line a 24 cm/9½ inch loose-bottomed quiche/flan tin (pan). Prick the pastry (pie dough) with a fork and chill for 30 minutes.

3 Line the pastry case (pie shell) with foil and baking beans and bake in a preheated oven, 190°C/375°F/ Gas Mark 5, for 15 minutes. Remove the foil and beans and cook for 15 minutes.

4 To make the filling, mix the orange rind, orange juice and breadcrumbs in a bowl. Stir in the lemon juice and cream. Melt the butter and sugar over a low heat. Remove the pan from

the heat, add the 2 egg yolks, salt and breadcrumb mixture and stir.

5 Whisk the egg whites with the salt until they form soft peaks. Fold them into the egg yolk mixture.

6 Pour the filling into the pastry case (pie shell). Bake in a preheated oven, 170°C/325°F/Gas 3, for about 45 minutes or until just set. Leave to cool slightly and serve warm.

Coconut Cream Tart

Serves 6–8

PASTRY (PIE DOUGH):
150 g/5^1/2 oz/1^1/4 cups plain
    (all-purpose) flour
25 g/1 oz/5 tsp caster
    (superfine) sugar
125 g/4^1/2 oz/^{1}/2 cup butter,
    cut into small pieces
1 tbsp water

FILLING:
425 ml/^{3}/4 pint/2 cups milk
125 g /4^1/2 oz creamed
    coconut
3 egg yolks
125 g/4^1/2 oz/^{1}/2 cup caster
    (superfine) sugar
50 g/1^3/4 oz/^{1}/2 cup plain (all-
    purpose) flour, sieved

25 g/1 oz/^{1}/3 cup desiccated
    (shredded) coconut
25 g/1 oz glacé (candied)
    pineapple, chopped, plus
    extra to decorate
2 tbsp rum or pineapple juice
300 ml/^{1}/2 pint/1^1/3 cups
    whipping cream, whipped,
    plus extra to decorate

1 Place the flour and sugar in a bowl and rub in the butter. Add the water and work the mixture together until a soft pastry (pie dough) has formed. Wrap and leave to chill for 30 minutes.

2 Roll out the dough and line a 24 cm/ 9½ inch loose-bottomed quiche/flan tin (pan). Prick the pastry with a fork and leave to chill for 30

minutes. Line the pastry case (pie shell) with foil and baking beans and bake in a preheated oven, 190°C/375°F/Gas 5, for 15 minutes. Remove the foil and beans and cook for a further 15 minutes. Leave to cool.

3 To make the filling, bring the milk and creamed coconut to just below boiling point, stirring to melt the coconut.

4 Whisk the egg yolks with the sugar until fluffy. Whisk in the flour. Add the hot milk, stirring. Return the mixture to the pan and gently heat for 8 minutes until thick, stirring. Leave to cool.

5 Stir in the coconut, pineapple and rum and spread the filling in the pastry case (pie shell). Cover with the whipped cream, decorate and chill.

White Chocolate & Almond Tart

Serves 8

INGREDIENTS

PASTRY (PIE DOUGH):
150 g/5 oz/1¼ cups plain (all-
   purpose) flour
25 g/1 oz/5 tsp caster
   (superfine) sugar
125 g/4½ oz/½ cup butter,
   cut into small pieces
1 tbsp water

FILLING:
150 g/5½ oz/½ cup golden
   (light corn) syrup
50 g/1¾ oz/10 tsp butter
75 g/2¾ oz/⅓ cup soft
   brown sugar
3 eggs, lightly beaten

100 g/3½ oz/½ cup whole
   blanched almonds, roughly
   chopped
100 g/3½ oz white chocolate,
   chopped roughly
cream, to serve (optional)

1 To make the pastry (pie shell), place the flour and sugar in a mixing bowl and rub in the butter with your fingers. Add the water and work the mixture together until a soft pastry (pie dough) has formed. Wrap and leave to chill for 30 minutes.

2 On a lightly floured surface, roll out the dough and line a 24 cm/ 9½ inch loose-bottomed quiche/flan tin (pan). Prick

the pastry (pie dough) with a fork and leave to chill for 30 minutes. Line the pastry case (pie shell) with foil and baking beans and bake in a preheated oven, 190°C/ 375°F/ Gas Mark 5, for 15 minutes. Remove the foil and baking beans and cook for a further 15 minutes.

3 To make the filling, gently melt the syrup, butter and sugar together in a saucepan. Remove from the heat and leave to cool

slightly. Stir in the beaten eggs, almonds and chocolate.

4 Pour the chocolate and nut filling into the prepared pastry case (pie shell) and cook in the oven for 30-35 minutes or until just set. Leave to cool before removing the tart from the tin (pan). Serve with cream, if wished.

Pina Colada Pineapple

Serves 4

INGREDIENTS

1 small pineapple
50 g/1³/4 oz unsalted butter
25 g/1 oz light muscovado
    sugar

50 g/1³/4 oz fresh coconut,
    grated
2 tbsp coconut-flavoured
    liqueur or rum

1 Using a very sharp knife, cut the pineapple into quarters and then remove the tough core from the centre, leaving the leaves attached.

2 Cut the pineapple flesh away from the skin. Make horizontal cuts across the flesh of the pineapple quarters.

3 Place the butter in a pan and heat gently until melted, stirring continuously. Brush the melted butter over the pineapple and sprinkle with the sugar.

4 Cover the pineapple leaves with kitchen foil in order to prevent them from burning and transfer them to a rack set over hot coals.

5 Barbecue (grill) the pineapple for about 10 minutes.

6 Sprinkle the coconut over the pineapple and barbecue (grill), cut side up, for a further 5–10 minutes or until the pineapple is piping hot.

7 Transfer the pineapple to serving plates and remove the foil from the leaves. Spoon a little coconut-flavoured liqueur or rum over the pineapple and serve immediately.

COOK'S TIP

Fresh coconut has the best flavour for this dish. If you prefer, however, you can use desiccated (shredded) coconut.

Stuffed Pears with Mincemeat

Serves 4

INGREDIENTS

4 firm pears	5 tbsp cake crumbs or 4	15 g/$^1/_2$ oz butter
1 tsp lemon juice	amaretti biscuits, crushed	ice cream, to serve
2 tbsp mincemeat		

1 Using a sharp knife, cut the pears in half. Using a teaspoon, scoop out the core and discard.

2 Brush the cut surface of each of the pear halves with a little lemon juice to prevent discoloration.

3 Mix together the mincemeat and cake crumbs or crushed amaretti biscuits.

4 Divide the mixture among the pear halves, spooning it into a mound where the core has been removed.

5 Place 2 pear halves on a large square of double thickness kitchen foil and generously dot all over with the butter.

6 Wrap up the foil around the pears so that they are enclosed.

7 Transfer the foil parcels to a rack set over hot coals. Barbecue (grill) for 25–30 minutes or until the pears are hot and just tender.

8 Transfer the pears to individual serving plates. Serve with 2 scoops of ice cream per serving.

VARIATION

Use mincemeat to stuff apples instead of pears and bake them on the barbecue (grill) in the same way.

COOK'S TIP

If the coals are dying down, place the kitchen foil parcels directly on to the coals and barbecue (grill) for 25–30 minutes.

Peaches with Creamy Mascarpone Filling

Serves 4

INGREDIENTS

4 peaches	40 g/1¹/₂ oz pecan or walnuts,	1 tsp sunflower oil
175 g/6 oz mascarpone cheese	chopped	4 tbsp maple syrup

1 Cut the peaches in half and remove the stones. If you are preparing this recipe in advance, press the peach halves together again and wrap them in cling film (plastic wrap) until required.

2 Mix the mascarpone and pecan or walnuts together in a small bowl until well combined. Leave to chill in the refrigerator until required.

3 To serve, brush the peaches with a little oil and place on a rack set over medium hot coals.

Barbecue (grill) the peach halves for 5–10 minutes, turning once, until hot.

4 Transfer the peach halves to a dish and top with the mascarpone and nut mixture.

5 Drizzle the maple syrup over the peaches and mascarpone filling and serve at once.

COOK'S TIP

Mascarpone cheese is high in fat; you can use thick natural yogurt instead.

VARIATION

You can use nectarines instead of peaches for this recipe, if you prefer. Remember to choose ripe but fairly firm fruit which won't go soft and mushy when it is barbecued (grilled). Prepare the nectarines in the same way as the peaches and barbecue (grill) for 5–10 minutes.

Banana Pastries

Serves 4

INGREDIENTS

DOUGH:
450 g/1 lb/4 cups plain (all-purpose) flour
60 g/2 oz/4 tbsp lard (shortening)
60 g/2 oz/4 tbsp unsalted butter

125 ml/4 fl oz/¹/₂ cup water
1 egg yolk, beaten
icing (confectioner's) sugar, for dusting
cream or ice cream, to serve

FILLING:
2 large bananas
75 g/2³/₄ oz/¹/₃ cup finely chopped no-need-to-soak dried apricots
pinch of nutmeg
dash of orange juice

1 To make the dough, sift the flour into a large mixing bowl. Add the lard (shortening) and butter and rub into the flour with the fingertips until the mixture resembles breadcrumbs. Gradually blend in the water to make a soft dough. Wrap in cling film (plastic wrap) and chill in the refrigerator for 30 minutes.

2 Mash the bananas in a bowl with a fork and stir in the apricots, nutmeg

and orange juice, mixing together well.

3 Roll the dough out on a lightly floured surface and cut out 16 × 10-cm/ 4-inch rounds.

4 Spoon a little of the banana filling on to one half of each round and fold the dough over the filling to make semi-circles. Pinch the edges together and seal them by pressing with the prongs of a fork.

5 Arrange the pastries on a non-stick baking tray (cookie sheet) and brush them with the beaten egg yolk.

6 Cut a small slit in each pastry and cook in a preheated oven, 180°C/ 350°F/Gas 4, for about 25 minutes, or until golden brown.

7 Dust with icing (confectioner's) sugar and serve with cream or ice cream.

Mango Mousse

Serves 4

INGREDIENTS

400 g/14 oz can mangoes in
    syrup
2 pieces stem (preserved)
    ginger, chopped

200 ml/7 fl oz/1 cup double
    (heavy) cream
20 g/³/4 oz/4 tsp powdered
    gelatine
2 tbsp water

2 egg whites
1¹/2 tbsp light brown sugar
stem (preserved) ginger and
    lime zest, to decorate

1 Drain the mangoes, reserving the syrup. Blend the mango pieces and ginger in a food processor or blender for 30 seconds, or until smooth.

2 Measure the purée and make up to 300 ml/¹/2 pint/1¹/4 cups with the reserved mango syrup.

3 In a separate bowl, whip the cream until it forms soft peaks. Fold the mango mixture into the cream until well combined.

4 Dissolve the gelatine in the water and leave to cool slightly. Pour the gelatine into the mango mixture in a steady stream, stirring constantly. Leave to cool in the refrigerator for about 30 minutes, until almost set.

5 Beat the egg whites in a clean bowl until they form soft peaks, then beat in the sugar. Gently fold the egg whites into the mango mixture with a metal spoon.

6 Spoon the mousse into individual serving

dishes and decorate with stem (preserved) ginger and lime zest. Serve immediately.

COOK'S TIP

*The gelatine must
be stirred into the mango
mixture in a gentle, steady
stream to prevent it from
setting in lumps when it
comes into contact with
the cold mixture.*

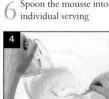

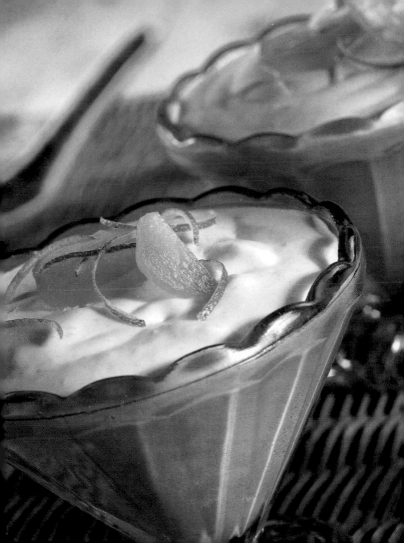

Chinese Custard Tarts

Makes 15

INGREDIENTS

DOUGH:
175 g/6 oz/1^{1}/2 cups plain
    (all-purpose) flour
3 tbsp caster (superfine) sugar
60 g/2 oz/4 tbsp unsalted
    butter

25 g/1 oz/2 tbsp lard
    (shortening)
2 tbsp water

CUSTARD:
2 small eggs

60 g/2 oz/^{1}/4 cup caster
    (superfine) sugar
175 ml/6 fl oz/^{3}/4 cup pint
    milk
^{1}/2 tsp ground nutmeg, plus
    extra for sprinkling
cream, to serve

1 To make the dough, sift the flour into a bowl. Add the sugar and rub in the butter and lard (shortening) until the mixture resembles breadcrumbs. Add the water and mix to form a dough.

2 Transfer the dough to a lightly floured surface and knead for 5 minutes, until smooth. Cover with cling film (plastic wrap) and leave to chill in the refrigerator while you prepare the filling.

3 To make the custard, beat the eggs and sugar together. Gradually add the milk and nutmeg and beat until well combined.

4 Separate the dough into 15 even-sized pieces. Flatten the dough pieces into rounds and press into shallow patty tins (pans).

5 Spoon the custard into the pastry cases (tart shells) and cook in a preheated oven, at 150°C/300°F/Gas Mark 2, for 25-30 minutes.

6 Transfer the tarts to a wire rack, leave to cool slightly, then sprinkle with nutmeg. Serve with cream.

COOK'S TIP

For extra convenience, make the dough in advance, cover and leave to chill in the refrigerator until required.

Battered Bananas

Serves 4

INGREDIENTS

8 medium bananas
2 tsp lemon juice
75 g/2³/4 oz/²/3 cup self-
    raising flour

75 g/2³/4 oz/²/3 cup rice flour
1 tbsp cornflour (cornstarch)
¹/2 tsp ground cinnamon
250 ml/8 fl oz/1 cup water

4 tbsp light brown sugar
oil, for deep-frying

1 Cut the bananas into chunks and place them in a large mixing bowl.

2 Sprinkle the lemon juice over the bananas to prevent discoloration.

3 Sift the self raising flour, rice flour, cornflour (cornstarch) and cinnamon into a mixing bowl. Gradually stir in the water to make a thin batter.

4 Heat the oil in a preheated wok until almost smoking, then reduce the heat slightly.

5 Place a piece of banana on the end of a fork and carefully dip it into the batter, draining off any excess. Repeat with the remaining banana pieces.

6 Sprinkle the sugar on to a large plate.

7 Carefully place the banana pieces in the oil and cook for 2-3 minutes, until golden. Remove the banana pieces from the oil with a slotted spoon and roll them in the sugar. Transfer to bowls and serve with cream or ice cream.

COOK'S TIP

Rice flour can be bought from wholefood shops or from Chinese supermarkets.

Almond Slices

Serves 6-8

INGREDIENTS

---

3 medium eggs
75 g/2³/4 oz/¹/2 cup ground
  almonds
200 g/7 oz/1¹/2 cups milk
  powder

200 g/7 oz/1 cup sugar
¹/2 tsp saffron strands
100 g/3¹/2 oz/8 tbsp unsalted
  butter

25 g/1 oz/1 tbsp flaked
  almonds

---

1 Beat the eggs together in a bowl and set aside.

2 Place the ground almonds, milk powder, sugar and saffron in a large mixing bowl and stir to mix well.

3 Melt the butter in a small saucepan.

4 Pour the melted butter over the dry ingredients and mix well with a fork.

5 Add the reserved beaten eggs to the almond mixture and stir to blend well.

6 Spread the mixture in a shallow 15-20 cm/ 7-9 inch ovenproof dish and bake in a pre-heated oven at 160°C/325°F/Gas Mark 3 for 45 minutes. Test whether the cake is cooked through by piercing with the tip of a knife or a skewer – it will come out clean if it is cooked thoroughly.

7 Once it had cooled, cut the almond cake into even slices.

8 Decorate the almond slices with flaked almonds and transfer them to serving plates. Serve hot or cold.

COOK'S TIP

These almond slices are best eaten hot but they may also be served cold. They can be made a day or even a week in advance and re-heated. They also freeze beautifully.

Pistachio Dessert

Serves 4-6

INGREDIENTS

850 ml/1^{1}/2 pints/3^{1}/2 cups
  water
250 g/9 oz/3 cups pistachio
  nuts
250 g/9 oz/1^{3}/4 cups full-
  cream dried milk powder

450 g/1 lb/2^{1}/3 cups sugar
2 cardamoms, with seeds
  crushed
2 tbsp rosewater
a few strands saffron

fresh mint leaves, to decorate

1 Boil about 1 pint/ 600 ml water in a saucepan. Remove the pan from the heat and soak the pistachios in this water for about 5 minutes. Drain and remove the skins.

2 Grind the pistachios in a food processor or pestle and mortar.

3 Add the dried milk powder to the ground pistachios and mix well.

4 To make the syrup, place the remaining

300 ml/^{1}/2 pint water and the sugar in a pan and heat gently. When the liquid begins to thicken, add the cardamom seeds, rosewater and saffron.

5 Add the syrup to the pistachio mixture and cook for about 5 minutes, stirring, until the mixture thickens. Set the mixture aside and leave to cool slightly.

6 Once cooled enough to handle, roll the mixture into balls (use up

all of the pistachio mixture). Decorate with a few fresh mint leaves and leave to set before serving.

COOK'S TIP

It is best to buy whole pistachio nuts and grind them yourself, rather than using packets of ready-ground nuts. Freshly ground nuts have the best flavour as grinding releases their natural oils.

Coconut Sweet

Serves 4-6

INGREDIENTS

75 g/2³/4 oz/6 tbsp butter
200 g/7 oz/3 cups desiccated
(shredded) coconut

175 ml/6 fl oz/³/4 cup
condensed milk

a few drops of pink food
colouring (optional)

1 Place the butter in a heavy-based saucepan and melt over a low heat, stirring so that the butter doesn't burn on the bottom of the pan.

2 Add the desiccated (shredded) coconut to the melted butter, stirring.

3 Stir in the condensed milk and the pink food colouring (if using) and mix continuously for 7-10 minutes.

4 Remove the saucepan from the heat, set aside and leave the coconut mixture to cool slightly.

5 Once cool enough to handle, shape the coconut mixture into long blocks and cut into equal-sized rectangles. Leave the sweet to set for about 1 hour, then serve.

VARIATION

If you prefer, you could divide the coconut mixture in step 2, and add the drops of pink food colouring to only one half of the mixture. This way, you will have an attractive combination of pink and white coconut sweets.

COOK'S TIP

Coconut is used extensively in Indian cooking to add flavour and creaminess to various dishes. The best flavour comes from freshly grated coconut, although ready-prepared dessicated (shredded) coconut, as used here, makes an excellent stand-by. Freshly grated coconut freezes successfully, so it is well worth preparing when you have the time.

Almond & Pistachio Dessert

Serves 4-6

INGREDIENTS

75 g/2³/4 oz/6 tbsp unsalted
   butter
200 g/7 oz/1 cup ground
   almonds

150 ml/5 fl oz/²/3 cup single
   (light) cream
200 g/7 oz/1 cup sugar
8 almonds, chopped

10 pistachio nuts, chopped

1 Place the butter in a medium-sized saucepan, preferably non-stick. Melt the butter, stirring well.

2 Gradually add the ground almonds, cream and sugar to the melted butter in the pan, stirring to combine. Reduce the heat and stir the mixture constantly for 10-12 minutes, scraping the bottom of the pan.

3 Increase the heat until the mixture turns a little darker in colour.

4 Transfer the almond mixture to a shallow serving dish and smooth the top with the back of a spoon.

5 Decorate the top of the dessert with the chopped almonds and pistachios.

6 Leave the dessert to set for about 1 hour, then cut into diamond shapes and serve cold.

COOK'S TIP

This almond dessert can be made in advance and stored in an airtight container in the refrigerator for several days.

COOK'S TIP

You could use a variety of shaped pastry cutters, to cut the dessert into different shapes, rather than diamonds, if you prefer.

Sweet Saffron Rice

Serves 4

INGREDIENTS

200 g/7 oz/1 cup basmati rice
200 g/7 oz/1 cup sugar
1 pinch saffron strands
300 ml/¹/₂ pint/1¹/₄ cups
    water

2 tbsp ghee
3 cloves
3 cardamoms
25 g/1 oz/2 tbsp sultanas

TO DECORATE:
a few pistachio nuts (optional)
varq (silver leaf) (optional)

1 Rinse the rice twice and bring to the boil in a saucepan of water, stirring. Remove the pan from the heat when the rice is half-cooked, drain the rice and set aside.

2 In a separate saucepan, boil the sugar and saffron in the water, stirring, until the syrup thickens. Set aside.

3 In another saucepan, heat the ghee, cloves and cardamoms, stirring occasionally. Remove the pan from the heat.

4 Return the rice to a low heat and add the sultanas, stirring well to combine.

5 Pour the syrup over the rice mixture and stir.

6 Pour the ghee mixture over the rice and leave to simmer over a low heat for 10-15 minutes. Check to see whether the rice is cooked; if not, add a little water, cover and leave to simmer gently.

7 Serve warm, decorated with pistachio nuts and *varq* (silver leaf), and with cream if desired.

VARIATION

For a slightly stronger saffron flavour, place the saffron strands on a small piece of kitchen foil and toast them lightly under a hot grill (broiler) for a few moments (take care not to overcook them or the flavour will spoil) and crush finely between your fingers before adding to the sugar and water in step 2.

This is a Parragon Book
First published in 2000
Parragon
Queen Street House
4 Queen Street
Bath BA1 1HE, UK

ISBN: 0-75253-374-6

Printed in China

Note

Cup measurements in this book are for American cups. Tablespoons are assumed to be
15 ml. Unless otherwise stated, milk is assumed to be full fat, eggs are medium and
pepper is freshly ground black pepper.